Technology Timelines

CAR

W
FRANKLIN WATTS
LONDON • SYDNEY

This edition first published in 2014
by Franklin Watts
338 Euston Road
London NW1 3BH

Franklin Watts Australia
Level 17/207 Kent Street
Sydney, NSW 2000

Copyright © 2014
Brown Bear Books Ltd

A CIP catalogue record for this book
is available from the British Library.

ISBN: 978-1-4451-3573-1
Dewey number: 629.2'22'09

Printed in China

Franklin Watts is a division of
Hachette Children's Books,
an Hachette UK company.
www.hachette.co.uk

Note to parents and teachers concerning
websites: In the book every effort has been
made by the Publishers to ensure that
websites are suitable for children, that they
are of the highest educational value, and that
they contain no inappropriate or offensive
material. However, because of the nature of
the Internet, it is impossible to guarantee that
the contents of these sites will not be altered.
We advise that Internet access is supervised
by a responsible adult.

Author: Tom Jackson
Designer: Lynne Lennon
Picture Researcher: Clare Newman
Children's Publisher: Anne O'Daly
Design Manager: Keith Davis
Editorial Director: Lindsey Lowe

Picture Credits
The photographs in this book are used by permission
and through the courtesy of:

Key: b = bottom, c = centre, is = insert , l = left,
mtg = montage, r = right, t = top.

Cover, main, tr, ll, ©Corbis; cover, tru, ©Thinkstock;
©Rob Wilson/Shutterstock.
Interior: 4tr, ©Ashwin/Shutterstock; 4cl, ©Morphart
Creation/Shutterstock; 4-5b, ©Thinkstock;
5t, © Anna Jurkovska/Shutterstock; 6b, ©Thinkstock;
6-7c, ©Wikipedia; 7t, ©Morphart Creation/
Shutterstock; 8b, ©Daimler Chrysler; 8-9t, ©Daimler
Chrysler; 9b, ©Look & Learn; 10b, ©Wikipedia;
10-11t, ©Rob Wilson/Shutterstock; 11tr, ©The Grang-
er Collection/Topham; 11b, ©Wikipedia;
12b, ©MEPL; 12-13c, ©Adiiano Castelli/Shutterstock;
13t, ©Padmayogini/Shutterstock; 13br, ©Library
of Congress; 14-15t, ©Sergey Kramshylin/
Shutterstock; 15tr, ©Thinkstock; 15bl, ©National Ar-
chives; 15br, ©Thurston Hopkins/Hulton Archive/Getty
Images; 16bl, ©Wikipedia; 16-17t,
©Shutterstock; 17cr, ©Wikipedia; 17br, ©Thomas
Dutour/Dreamstime; 18bc, ©Nature Photos/
Shutterstock; 18-19t, ©Bright/Shutterstock;
19cr, ©NASA; 19bl, ©Wikipedia; 20bl ©Thinkstock;
20-21t, ©Daimler Chrysler; 21tc, ©Corbis News/
Corbis; 21br, ©Shutterstock; 23tr, ©Boris Rabtsauel/
Shutterstock; 23bl, ©Sergey Peterman/Shutterstock;
23br, ©John Evans/Shutterstock; 24-25t, ©d13/
Shutterstock; 25bl, ©Liane M/Shutterstock;
25br, ©Drayton Racing; 26-27c, ©Stuart Elflett/
Shutterstock; 27tr, ©Thinkstock; 27br, ©The
BLOODHOUND Project; 28bl, ©Pascal Goetcheluck/
SPL; 28-29t, ©Alain Benainous/Gamma Ralpho/Getty
Images; 29bl, ©Shi Yali/Shutterstock; 29br, ©Stefan
Redel/Shutterstock.

Brown Bear Books has made every attempt
to contact the copyright holder.
If you have any information please contact
licensing@brownbearbooks.co.uk

Contents

Introduction

The car was invented more than a century ago. Now there are one billion of them on the world's roads. Long before cars, people were building roads and travelling in other vehicles. The wheel was invented about 6,000 years ago. In place of an engine, vehicles were hauled along roads by animals.

Egyptian chariot

The first high-speed vehicle was the chariot, a two-wheeled carriage pulled by a horse. It was invented about 4,000 years ago, and was used by soldiers in ancient Egypt.

HERON OF ALEXANDRIA

In the 1st century C.E. an Egyptian named Heron invented a machine called the aeolipile. It used jets of steam to spin a ball. Heron used his gadget as a toy, but he realised it could also be used to power machines. That makes the aeolipile the first engine.

« POWER PEOPLE »

Road networks

The ancient empires of Rome and Persia had many roads. They were flat and straight, and they were the fastest way to get around. The roads were paved with stones so that heavy carts and columns of marching soldiers did not sink into the soft ground.

Stagecoach

Before the car was invented the fastest way to travel was by stagecoach. The first stagecoach services began in Britain in the 1640s. As its name suggests, the coach made each journey in stages. The coach stopped off at 'staging posts' to get fresh horses – and collect letters, or the 'post'.

Under Steam

The first self-propelled vehicle was a massive three-wheeled wagon powered by a steam engine. It was built in 1769 by French inventor Nicolas Cugnot. On its first journey the carriage hit a wall in what was the world's first traffic accident!

Cugnot's vehicle was designed as a gun carriage for hauling heavy guns across muddy battlefields. It had a top speed of 4 km/h (2.5 mph), about as fast as a person walks, but the engine ran out of coal in just 15 minutes.

Steaming ahead

The steam engine hung at the front. A jet of steam flowing out of the boiler pushed two pistons up and down. This motion then turned the front wheel, pushing the carriage forward.

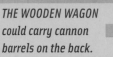

THE WOODEN WAGON could carry cannon barrels on the back.

LARGE BACK WHEELS could roll across rough ground.

TIMELINE

1500s
Suspension
Craftsmen in Kocs, Hungary, build wagons that hang between the wheels, so they bounce less on bumpy roads. They are named the *kocsi*, or coach.

1698
Steam pump
English inventor Thomas Savery makes the first steam engine. It was used to pump water out of mines (right).

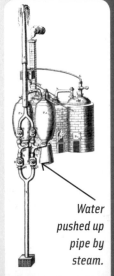

Water pushed up pipe by steam.

1801
Puffing Devil
Englishman Richard Trevithick, drives his steam-powered car called Puffing Devil through the Cornish town of Camborne.

THE DRIVER steered by using a lever to move the front wheel.

EDGAR HOOLEY

In the 1800s, roads were covered in loose gravel. For a smooth ride, drivers had to wait until 1901, when Englishman Edgar Hooley covered the stones in tar, making hard, dust-free 'tarmac'.

A PIPE carried steam to the pistons.

A COAL-FIRED FURNACE heated a tank of water to produce a supply of high-pressure steam.

THE PISTONS were connected to the front wheel.

1832
Differential gear
A cog system allows the wheels on one axle to turn at different speeds, making it easier to turn sharp corners.

Left wheel can spin more slowly than right one when vehicle turns left.

Smaller cogs allow the wheels to spin separately.

Large cog is used to drive wheels in powered vehicle.

1862
Internal Combustion
Étienne Lenoir from Belgium builds a cart that is powered by a flammable gas that burns inside the engine – the first internal combustion engine.

7

Horseless Carriage

The first car was built in 1885 by the German engineer Karl Benz. It was a tricycle powered by a four-stroke internal combustion engine.

Combustion means 'burning', and the power of an internal combustion engine comes from burning fuel, such as petrol, inside containers called cylinders. Each cylinder is fitted with a piston that can slide up and down inside. The fuel is squeezed and makes little explosions inside the cylinders. The explosions push down on the pistons, and the moving pistons make the wheels spin.

Benz Viktoria

This model was built in 1893. Its wheels and body were like the ones used on horse-drawn vehicles. No one called them cars back back then. Instead the vehicles were known as 'horseless carriages'.

TIMELINE

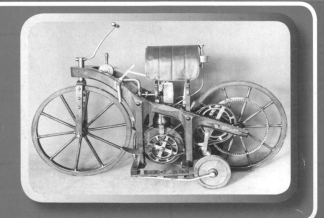

1885
First motorcycle
German Gottlieb Daimler invents the motorcycle, a few months before the first car is built.

1887
Air-filled tyres
Scottish inventor John Dunlop fits his son's tricycle with rubber tubes filled with air to make them hard. Soon cars are being fitted with air-filled tyres.

THE DRIVER steered with a small wheel on an upright column.

FOUR-STROKE CYCLE

An engine's pistons make four up and down movements, or strokes, in a repeating cycle. The cycle begins with fuel entering the cylinder, it is then squeezed, burned and the waste, or exhaust, is expelled.

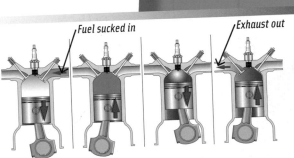

Fuel sucked in   Exhaust out

STROKE 1: Piston drops.

STROKE 2: Piston rises, squeezing fuel.

STROKE 3: Fuel burns, pushing down piston.

STROKE 4: Piston rises, pushing out exhaust.

The up and down motion of the pistons is converted to a spinning motion by the crankshaft.

THE FRONT WHEELS were smaller than the back wheels. This was the same system used on horse-drawn carriages.

1892

Diesel engine

Rudolph Diesel invents an engine fuelled by heavier oil than petrol. The fuel burns when compressed rather than being set alight by a spark as in petrol engines.

1896

Red flags

The 1865 law saying that cars in Britain must have warning flags carried in front of them is ended. The speed limit goes up from 3 km/h (2 mph) to 23 km/h (14 mph).

Mass Production

When American businessman Henry Ford set up his car company in 1903, each of his cars was built by hand. A few years later he developed a way of making cars more quickly and cheaply. By 1920 half the cars in the world were made by Ford.

Ford's cars were built on an assembly line, where teams of workers added one set of components to each car. The car then moved to the next team to add the next set of components. The Ford factory in Detroit produced 14,000 cars a week!

Ford Model T

There were 15 million Model Ts built between 1908 and 1927. This was the first car that ordinary people could afford, costing about four months' salary.

THE OPEN ROOF made the Model T cheaper to produce.

THE WHEELS were made of wood and were based on the wheels used to move heavy guns.

TIMELINE

1901

Mercedes cars
Emil Jellinek, the owner of the Daimler company, decides to name all the firm's new cars Mercedes after one of his daughters.

1903

Driving test
The first compulsory driving test is introduced in Prussia, now part of Germany.

1904

Flaming lights
Headlights that burn the gas acetylene are introduced. Electric headlights arrive in 1908.

THE ENGINE was powered by petrol, kerosene, or alcohol.

AIR PRESSURE in the tyres was higher than those on a modern car, meaning they burst more easily.

THE LIGHTS only worked when the engine was on.

A HAND CRANK was turned to get the engine moving until the pistons started to rise and fall on their own.

1913

Assembly line
Before the assembly line was introduced in 1913, a Ford took six hours to build. By 1925 the assembly line was making one car every ten minutes.

1916

Windscreen wipers
Wipers powered by an air pump in the engine are introduced. Hand-powered windscreen wipers had been patented in the United States by Mary Anderson in 1903.

Sports Car

As engines became more powerful in the 1920s, driving cars became more fun. Small, fast cars were built for driving in the countryside. Today we call them sports cars.

The first sports cars were based on car models designed for racing. They generally had just two seats and no roof. The early name for these cars was roadsters but by the 1920s they were being used for 'sport', or for fun, and became 'sports cars'.

Jaguar SS100

Jaguar is a famous make of sports cars. Early models were made by SS Cars. One model from 1936 was called the SS100 because it could reach speeds of 160 km/h (100 mph). In the 1930s, the sleek SS cars were renamed Jaguars and the company eventually took that name as well.

THE ENGINE only filled the rear section of the bonnet, which was made longer so the car looked more sleek and powerful.

A BATTERY supplied electricity for the lights and to start the engine at the push of a button.

TIMELINE

1919
Brake pedal
A single pedal is used to slow and stop the car, using brakes on all four wheels. Before then drivers had to use a foot pedal and a hand lever at the same time.

1922
Traffic lights
The first automatic traffic lights with red, amber and green lights on a timer are installed in Houston, Texas, in the United States.

Even in 1930 people were interested in old cars. The Veteran Car Club was set up in Brighton, England to make sure that older models of car were saved. Every year members show off the cars on a drive from London to Brighton.

« A DIFFERENT VIEW »

THE WINDSCREEN folded down to reduce drag at high speeds.

THE CURVED MUD GUARDS reminded people of a crouching cat, so the model was named the Jaguar.

THE LIGHTWEIGHT WHEELS had wire spokes like a bicycle wheel.

1926
Power steering
The first car fitted with power steering is introduced. It uses hydraulic pumps to move the front wheels.

1930s
Motorways
High-speed intercity roads used only by cars and other motorised vehicles are opened in Europe and America.

1935
Flashing indicators
The first flashing lights to signal that a car is turning are developed in America.

Going Off Road

In World War II (1939–45), armies wanted tough vehicles that could drive over rough ground. The result was the four-wheel drive Jeep.

Most cars are two-wheel drive, which means the engine is connected to just two wheels. This works fine on smooth roads, but cars can get stuck on rough, slippery ground if the two powered wheels cannot grip anything. Vehicles with four-wheel drive, where the engine turns all four wheels, do not get stuck so easily, because there are twice as many wheels pushing them along.

US Army Jeep

Jeep was the nickname for the GP vehicle (short for 'general purpose'). This tough four-wheel drive car was introduced in 1941.

THE BUMPER stuck out in front to knock down obstacles like shrubs, fences and barbed wire.

THE WINDSCREEN folded flat so soldiers could shoot forward while driving along.

TIMELINE

1940

Automatic gears
Oldsmobile built the first car with a fully automatic gearbox that adjusts the gears as the car changes speed.

A pump system changes gear depending on engine speed.

The gears wheels are arranged in a ring.

Power to wheels.

1942

The 'Duck'
The US Army DUKW truck is designed to drive on land but float in water and operate like a powerboat.

THE SEAT CUSHIONS have compartments for storing maps and documents.

HANDLES AND HOOKS were useful for towing things and hoisting the Jeep on to ships or aircraft.

Gun turret can swing all the way around.

Room for crew of four inside.

Caterpillar track

« INSIDE OUT »

THE TANK

The toughest military vehicles of all use a different design. A tank's caterpillar tracks can drive across ground too rough for even four-wheel drive cars. The tank steers by driving the track on one side faster than on the other. As a result the tank spins around.

THE BODY is high off the ground so rocks do not get stuck underneath.

THE TYRES have a thick tread that allows the wheel to keep a grip on loose ground like mud, and sand.

1945

VW Beetle
Named after its curved shape, this German model, designed during World War II, is the most successful small car of all time. Modern versions are still manufactured today.

Cars for Everyone

After World War II, a lot of people wanted to own a car but could not afford to buy one. So companies began to build small cars that did not cost very much money to run.

The new type of vehicle was called the 'economy car'. They were designed to be useful to families living in cities as well as to people living in the countryside. The cars were often developed by governments who were keen to get their people on the move.

Citroen 2CV

The Citroën 2CV was produced from 1948 to 1990. In total nearly 3.5 million were made. The 2CV is short for 'deux chevaux', which is French for 'two horsepower', the power of the car's small engine.

WINDSCREEN WIPER speed was linked to how fast the car was going.

THE DIRECTION of the headlights could be adjusted so they always point at the road.

THE ENGINE was at the front and was kept cool by the air rushing over it.

TIMELINE

1947
First Ferrari
The 125s was the first car built by the Italian Ferrari company. The racing car won nearly half of its races in 1947.

1948
Cruise control
An electrical sensor adjusts the speed of the engine to keep the wheels turning at the same rate.

1950
Jet car
The British car firm Rover builds JET1, the first car powered by a gas turbine, the same system used in jet engines.

THE SUNROOF was made of fabric that could be rolled back.

THE WINDOWS did not roll down, but opened out as flaps.

THE TYRES AND SUSPENSION were designed for driving over fields as well as on roads.

THE MESSERSCHMITT BUBBLE CAR

This 1950s 'microcar' had room for two people, one sitting behind the other. There were two wheels at the front but only one at the back!

« A DIFFERENT VIEW »

1958
Glass fibre
The Lotus Elite becomes the first car to have a body made of lightweight glass-fibre, rather than sheets of metal.

1959
The Mini
Britain's famous Mini is introduced. It was 3 m long but still had room for four people. Nearly two million were built over 40 years, including a high-speed version called the Mini Cooper.

Long-Distance Luxury

As networks of high-speed roads and motorways were built across many countries, big cars were designed for making long-distance journeys in comfort and style.

By the 1960s cars had become more comfortable and easier to drive. This was most important in North America, where drivers made long journeys in big cars like this Cadillac. Automatic gearboxes became standard in the US. All a driver had to do was speed up, slow down and steer. Electric windows became common, and petrol-powered air-conditioners kept the car at just the right temperature.

CHROME, a shiny form of steel that did not rust, was used to decorate the car.

TIMELINE

1961
Safety checks
A compulsory yearly Ministry of Transport (MOT) test is introduced in the UK to check that older cars are safe enough to travel on the road.

1970
Seat belts
Australia becomes the first place to make it illegal to drive without a seat belt.

1973
Flying car
American Henry Smolinski connects the wings of a small aircraft to a Ford Pinto to make the Mizar, a road car that can also fly.

A HARDTOP, or permanent metal roof, only became a normal feature in the 1950s.

THE SLEEK TAILFINS were inspired by the shape of fighter planes.

« A DIFFERENT VIEW »

LUNAR ROVER

In 1971 a car was taken to the Moon for the first time. The battery-powered rover steered using both the front and back wheels, so the astronauts could make quick turns. The tyres were not filled with air but were made from woven metal wires.

A RADIO was fitted to the dashboard to provide music.

'WHITEWALL' TYRES used expensive white rubber to give the car a luxury look.

1976 ➤
Crash-test dummy
The Hybrid Family of five crash-test dummies are developed to match the weight and size of average humans – a man, woman and three children.

1979 ➤
People carrier
Early models of a large passenger vehicle, the size of van but with space inside for seven people, are developed in France.

Improving Safety

Towards the end of the 1900s, people realised that cars caused many problems. New laws forced car manufacturers to produce cleaner and safer models.

A CRASH TEST checks how the bonnet collapses. It is designed with 'crumple room', meaning it is squashed in the crash, while the passenger cabin stays undamaged.

Burning petrol produces mainly steam and carbon dioxide, but it also releases specks of soot and poisonous gases. By the 1980s air pollution from cars was creating clouds of pollution, called smog, around big cities. Catalytic converters were fitted to exhaust pipes to remove most of the worst pollution.

Crash test

Cars designed before the 1980s were not as safe as today. It was more common for passengers to die in crashes. New vehicles are now tested to see what happens when they crash. They are designed to protect the people inside the car during an accident.

TIMELINE

1981
Catalytic converters
A platinum-coated grill converts poisons in exhaust into into less harmful nitrogen, carbon dioxide and steam.

Brake

1985
Anti-Lock brakes
A speed sensor makes all wheels brake at the same rate to prevent skidding.

1989
Keyless entry
A transmitter fitted inside the key sends a radio signal to the electric-powered door locks. The car can be opened and closed by just pressing buttons on the key.

A DUMMY driver moves like a real person during a real crash.

THE WINDOWS have plastic coverings so the glass in between does not shatter when cracked.

RECLAIM THE STREETS

In the 1990s, people began to complain that there were too many cars. Heavy traffic made cities unpleasant. Protesters all over the world 'reclaimed the streets' by holding parties and picnics in the middle of the road.

« A DIFFERENT VIEW »

THE MEASUREMENT BAR shows testers exactly how the car changes shape during the crash.

DURING A CRASH, the passenger area should stay undamaged thanks to a safety cage of strong bars around it.

1991
Speed cameras
Automatic cameras that bounce a laser off passing cars to measure their speed are introduced in the UK. They photograph cars driving at unsafe speeds.

1998
Airbags
Safety gas-filled cushions that inflate when a car stops very suddenly – perhaps in a crash – are included as standard in all new cars.

Computer Control

The cars of the 21st century are safer and more efficient than ever. They use computers to control the engine and help with driving.

The first dashboards were on horse-drawn carriages. They were panels placed in front of the driver to stop stones kicked up by a horse's hooves from hitting passengers. Today, the dashboard is a car's control centre. It is fitted with indicators and switches and there is often a computer screen used to give directions, control the music player and even give a camera's view from the back of the car!

Family car

A modern car is made of about 14,000 parts. The body is made from several shaped steel and plastic panels bolted together.

HEADRESTS protect the head and neck if the car is hit from behind.

THE FUEL TANK is under the car. A floating sensor inside checks the level, which is shown on a dashboard indicator.

THE SUSPENSION uses large springs to absorb any bumps in the road.

TIMELINE

2000
Accurate sat nav
The full GPS signal is made available to non-military systems. This makes accurate in-car navigation kits possible.

2001
On-board computer
All petrol cars made in Europe are built with a computer system that records any faults in the engine and other important systems, and alerts the driver with warning lights.

2003
Hands-free law
A new law says that all phone calls have to be made using a hands-free headset while driving.

THE SUNROOF lets more natural light into the car.

THE DASHBOARD has indicators showing how the car is performing.

HOW SAT NAV WORKS

A satellite navigation (or sat nav) system uses 32 satellites moving around Earth in precise orbits. The satellites give out radio signals, which are picked up by a car's sat nav. The sat nav then calculates where it is by figuring out the distance to the three nearest satellites.

A STANDARD engine has four cylinders in a row. Modern designs have fuel injectors, which pump the fuel into the cylinders.

2005

Plate recognition

Cameras that can read the licence plate of speeding cars are set up along all major roads in the UK.

Increasing Efficiency

Cars are a major source of carbon dioxide. This gas is changing the atmosphere and is thought to be affecting the weather around the world. The very latest cars produce little or no carbon dioxide at all.

THE BATTERY AND MOTOR are at the back of the car.

One way to reduce carbon dioxide is to burn less petrol, and the way to do that is to make car engines more efficient so that cars can travel further on each tank of fuel. The latest petrol fuel burns better so less is wasted. Biofuels are also mixed into it. Biofuels are made from plants and so do not add extra carbon dioxide to the air.

Smart ED

Electric cars, like this 2013 two-seater, are good for driving in cities. However, they are slower than petrol cars and run out of power on long journeys.

TIMELINE

2007
Robot car race
A race for driverless cars is held on an old military base in California. Robot cars had to complete a 96-km (60 miles) course in less than six hours.

2008
Parktronics
Parking sensors become common in cars. High-pitched sounds echo off objects near the car and warn the driver if they get too close while parking.

2010
Liquid gas fuel
Autogas, a liquid fuel made from chilled natural gas, becomes generally available. The fuel produces less pollution than petrol or diesel.

THE TWO-PERSON car is small and light and so does not need a lot of power.

THE ELECTRIC ENGINE is very quiet. A warning buzz is given to alert pedestrians when the car is about to move.

THE BATTERY has to be plugged in for several hours to recharge.

ELECTRIC CARS produce no waste, and so have no exhaust pipe.

HYBRID CAR

A hybrid car uses a petrol engine for high speeds and an electric motor for slow driving. Energy recovery systems make electricity from the brakes. This is used to charge up a battery and make hybrids cars very efficient compared to petrol-only ones.

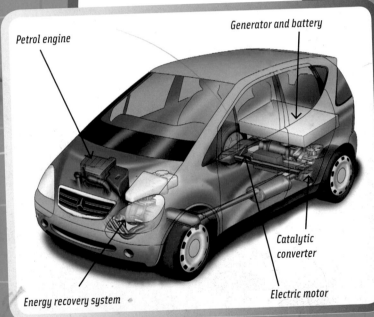

Petrol engine

Generator and battery

Catalytic converter

Electric motor

Energy recovery system

2013

Electric record

The Lola Drayson B12/69 EV sets a new speed record for an electric car: 328.6 km/h (204.2 mph) at a race track in England.

The Need For Speed

Many advances in car technology come from racing cars. Racing cars are not designed for comfort or efficiency, they are built to go fast and win races.

Racing cars, such as this 2005 Formula 1 Grand Prix car, are built to run on tracks at speeds three or four times faster than normal road cars – and sometimes faster than a small aircraft. At such high speeds, air resistance is a problem. The air pushes back on the car as it moves forward. As a result, F1 racing cars sit very close to the ground and are shaped like a wedge so they can slice through the air.

A CAMERA is fitted to the car to give fans a driver's eye view of the race.

INTAKES take in the air needed to burn the fuel in the engine.

THE COCKPIT is a very tight fit. The steering wheel comes off to make it easier for the driver to get in and out.

THE NOSE section can be replaced quickly if it is damaged in a collision.

WINGS on the front and back of the car work in the opposite way to an aircraft wings. They push the car down onto the track.

WIND TUNNEL

All cars, not just racers, need to be aerodynamic to cut through the air easily. This is tested in a wind tunnel. A stream of smoke shows how air moves around the car.

THE ENGINE of a Formula 1 car is a standard size to make races fair. They have turbos, which are fans blown around by the exhaust gas. The fan then pumps extra fuel and air into the engine.

ANDY GREEN

The world's fastest driver is Andy Green, a British fighter pilot. In 1997, Andy was the first person to drive faster than the speed of sound in his jet-powered car Thrust SSC. He is planning to go even faster in Bloodhound (below), which has a rocket engine as well as a jet.

« POWER PEOPLE »

THE TYRES are made from soft rubber that clings to the track.

FAST FORWARD

The Future of Driving

Today's cars are very different to the first Benz from the 1880s. In the future, cars will change all over again. We may travel in cars that give out only steam in the exhaust and even let a computer do the driving.

By 2050 there might be 2.5 billion cars – and that will produce a lot of traffic jams. To keep traffic moving cars may form trains, or 'platoons', linked by computer. Another way to reduce car numbers is to share them. When finished, a person just parks and leaves the car for the next driver.

Driverless car

Cars that drive by themselves use radar to create a map of all the objects in the area – including other cars and pedestrians. The computer then steers around the objects safely, while the passengers sit back and relax.

One of a kind

Concept cars are unique vehicles that show a new idea in car design. For example, the BMW Gina has a flexible skin instead of a metal covering. The frame inside can be adjusted to change the car's shape. The bonnet does not lift up, but folds out to reveal the engine.

« INSIDE OUT »

FUEL CELLS

A fuel cell is a power source that makes electricity out of hydrogen and oxygen. The only waste produced is harmless steam. A car powered by a fuel cell gives out no pollution.

Solar-powered car

Racing cars have been built that run on electricity generated from sunlight. These solar cars are still very flimsy. However, solar panels can be added to normal cars to top up engine power.

Glossary

ancient Egypt A civilisation that lived in Egypt starting around 6,000 years ago.

automatic When something happens on its own without a person having to control it.

carbon dioxide An invisible gas produced when most fuels burn.

combustion Another word for burning.

component A pre-made part, which is combined with others to make a larger machine.

crank A crooked handle used to spin a shaft by hand.

cylinder A circular container; car engines can have between four and sixteen cylinders. Fuel is burned inside them.

diesel A type of engine fuel similar to petrol, only it is thicker and does not burn as easily.

gas turbine A system of fans that burns a fuel to create a jet of gas. The jet of gas makes the fans spin around even faster.

glass fibre Flexible strands of glass that can be moulded into different shapes. When heated the glass fibres melt together to form a single object.

GPS Short for Global Positioning System, the technology used by most sat nav devices.

hydraulic Operated by the force of liquids pushing through tubes.

Persia Part of the Middle East now covered mainly by Iran. Persia ruled a huge empire about 2,500 years ago.

piston A moving rod or lever that slides up and down inside a cylinder. A car's pistons move when pushed by the hot expanding gases produced by burning the fuel.

pressure A measure of how hard a force is pushing on an object.

Rome The capital of Italy and once the centre of a huge empire around 2,000 years ago.

salary The money a person earns in one year.

vehicle A machine used for transporting people and cargo.

Further Resources

Books

Car Crazy. Dorling Kindersley, 2012.

Car Science, Richard Hammond. Dorling Kindersley, 2012.

Draw 50 Cars, Trucks, and Motorcycles, Lee J. Ames. Watson-Guptill, 2012.

Know it All: Cars, Andrew Langley. Franklin Watts, 2014.

Racing Driver: How to Drive Racing Cars Step by Step. Thames and Hudson Ltd, 2014.

To the Limit: Fantastically Fast Cars, Jim Pipe. Franklin Watts, 2014.

World's Fastest Cars (Haynes Pocket Manual), Richard Dredge. J H Haynes & Co Ltd, 2010.

Websites

http://auto.howstuffworks.com/car.htm
A HowStuffWorks guide to how everything on a car works from the engine to the electric windows.

http://www.history.com/topics/automobiles
Videos and facts about the history of the automobile from the History Channel.

http://animagraffs.com/how-a-car-engine-works
An animated guide to how an internal combustion engine works.

http://www.toyota.co.jp/en/kids/eco/anime_hyb.html
A fun guide to how Toyota's hybrid cars and other pollution-busting technology works.

http://www.formula1.com/video
Take a drive in a Formula 1 car and see what the driver sees. (Registration required.)

http://www.bloodhoundssc.com
Get all the facts and figures behind the fastest car the world has ever seen.

Index